Amazing!

Creative Recipes from *Changed* Choices CARE I

Changed **Choices**
Building new lives beyond prison walls

Outskirts Press, Inc.
http://www.outskirtspress.com

ISBN: 978-1-9772-4148-1

Cover Photo © 2021 pexels.com. All rights reserved - used with permission.
Cover designer - Victoria Belle-Miller
Contributors: Changed Choices CARE I Women
Compiled by: Catherine Kozlinski, Ruth Snyder

Outskirts Press and the "OP" logo are trademarks belonging to Outskirts Press, Inc.

PRINTED IN THE UNITED STATES OF AMERICA

May the recipes in this book nourish you and lift your spirit as your love has done for me. I appreciate you!

~~Violet

Table of Contents

I am glad that you are brave enough to try our recipes and I hope you enjoy them.

~~Pennie

Dedication

This book is dedicated to the Staff and Volunteers of Changed Choices.
The sentiments of the CARE I Women are found here and throughout the book.

Thank you to all of the beautiful staff and volunteers of Changed Choices. You have prayed for me and been a source of encouragement and inspiration in my life. I also pray in return for each and every one of you when I receive your letters. This way we remain in prayer and communication with our Lord Jesus. Thank you from the bottom of my heart for your genuine love

~~Ivonne

To the staff and volunteers who make it possible for Changed Choices to function: thank you. Your selflessness, caring, dedication, and hard work touch more people than you can ever know. The real-world impact of what you do and how you do it has made a difference in my life, both inside and out, whether it's just simply getting mail, having a wonderful place to go when I get out, or knowing I'm being lifted up in prayer by women of God. You are appreciated, prayed-for, and loved. Thank you!

~~Jessica

Changed Choices has impacted me in such a positive way. Every day they continue to make a difference in my life. I want this dedication for you because the staff and volunteers are so supportive and have given me a new purpose. I will forever be grateful. "*Those who hope in the Lord will renew their strength.*" Isaiah 40:31

~~Candice

You gave me hope for a future, which I did not have before. You keep my spirits lifted because I don't really have anyone else.

~~Heather

I thank all of you who are a part of Changed Choices (both staff and volunteers) for all your letters and the way you have uplifted me. It means the world to me; makes me do and be a better person and lets me know that my past does not define me.

~~Maria

Thank you, staff and volunteers for what you do. I pray that Changed Choices will continue to do what you do for us and for those on the outside. I am happy to be a part of Changed Choices. Thank you for your prayers.

~~Mary

Changed Choices
Building new lives beyond prison walls

Acknowledgements

This book is truly a collaborative effort that demonstrates the unity and supportive nature of the Changed Choices family. It was designed as a surprise for the new Pre-Release Manager, Lindsay Knuckles, but evolved into a thank you for all staff and volunteers who make Changed Choices a unique and thriving organization. While compiling the recipes, it became clear that the volunteers hold a very special place in the hearts of all CARE I women, who are so appreciative of the many ways the volunteers encourage and support them.

The people responsible for the content of this book are the women of Changed Choices CARE I who have shared their recipes with us as a token of their desire to give back what has so freely been given to them. Our women are indeed a resourceful, intelligent, determined and creative group, whose recipes are a demonstration of those gifts and abilities. From the very beginning there was excitement and the pooling of recipes and ideas resulting in what you are now holding. A tremendous amount of admiration and respect is due the women you will meet in this book.

The book would not have come together without the time consuming and diligent work of Cathy Kozlinski, who typed up the recipes and arranged them in an appealing manner for the reader. As a Changed Choices volunteer herself, she has made possible something that CARE I could only have dreamed of. Cathy found herself enjoying the personalities of the contributors as she worked on putting into print the ideas and recipes sent to her.

Victoria Belle-Miller, another Changed Choices volunteer, used her creative gift on the cover design. Tori took the time from her busy schedule to add this vital component to the collaboration.

The volunteers and staff have all worked hard over the years to see that I was encouraged. You all stood in the gap for me while I was waiting for parole to answer! It takes a village, a community of people working together, with the same goals to create the recipe for success! I am spiritually, emotionally, mentally etc. where I am today because of you "**ALL!**"

~~Dravia

Introduction

When you find yourself a part of the prison system with no access to a normal kitchen, the creative and innovative juices begin to flow. A microwave is the only stove and normal kitchen utensils are not available or allowed. The only food items available are what happen to be in the facility canteen (store) or in a food box sent periodically by a family member through a prison approved specific company that includes only predetermined items. The canteen items are available on a rotation basis with different items being available for sale at different times; each facility runs the canteen in a different way. Items are sold in "bundles" such as five packets of mayo in a bundle etc. A county Detention Center does not have a microwave or many of the food items. Beyond all this, it is resourceful, inspired and talented women who are able to create food for celebrations, relaxation or simply something that reminds them of home.

Food is one of the most powerful tools for building connections. The preparation of the foods presented in this book is usually done bringing several women together to celebrate birthdays, upcoming release dates or simply as an opportunity to share together. This community effort allows for the sense of family and normalcy. Overall, food brings us together as a human race; it brings us together to fellowship, show love, learn, and eat good food. This is an important part of life for CARE I women as they share with each other and now with you.

When creating these dishes, several adaptations were needed:

- Shred cheese using a plastic fork or spork.
- Use a plastic knife or a prison ID card to slice.
- Cookies can be crushed using the top of a mayo or barbecue sauce plastic "jar".
- Cup cheese is soft cheese that comes from the food box.
- Although some of the quantities listed are vague, "ex-offenders know the measurements automatically".
- Packets of meat and sauces may be purchased from the canteen.
- Noodles are usually Ramen noodles.
- Seasoning is primarily the seasoning packet in Ramen noodles.
- Items such as ice-cream may be available occasionally from the canteen.

I am glad to be a part of a wonderful creation!

~ ~Lataurus

The staff and volunteers of Changed Choices offer us something a lot of us have never experienced – unconditional love. They are there with a kind word or just a simple, "I'm praying for you". Each of you is a blessing to me.

~ ~ Brenda

Breakfast

To all the staff and volunteers: You helped me grow and to change. You helped me learn to love God more and to love myself more. Now we can learn from each other and share with each other through the recipes in this cookbook.

~ ~Latasha

All of you take time out of your busy lives to help someone like me to get my life back on track, and I am truly grateful for my entire Changed Choices family.

~ ~Veronica

Changed **Choices**
Building new lives beyond prison walls

Breakfast Pizza

INGREDIENTS:
- Tortilla
- Powdered eggs
- Block cheese
- Sausage

DIRECTIONS:
1. Place tortilla in microwave for 30 seconds to make it crisp.
2. Mix eggs with water according to directions.
3. Shred cheese – enough to cover tortilla.
4. Cut sausage into small pieces, enough for tortilla.
5. Spread eggs, cheese, and sausage over tortilla.
6. Place in microwave for 20-30 seconds to melt.

~~Ronda

Breakfast Sweet Wraps

INGREDIENTS:

- 2 flour tortilla wraps
- 1 package of mayonnaise
- 1 package cappuccino
- 1 package cocoa
- 2 packets sugar

DIRECTIONS:

1. Spread ½ package mayonnaise evenly over a tortilla.
2. Rub the second tortilla over the first to spread the mayo on it as well.
3. Lay each tortilla flat on a paper towel or paper plate.
4. Sprinkle cappuccino, cocoa, or sugar, over each tortilla. (You can use a combination of these, or all 3).
5. Put each tortilla into the microwave for 45 seconds to a minute until crispy.
6. Cool and eat.

You will have a wonderful sweet and crispy treat!

~~Dawn

Breakfast Wrap

INGREDIENTS:

- Tortilla
- Powdered eggs
- Block cheese
- Sausage

DIRECTIONS:

1. Mix eggs according to directions.
2. Cut cheese into small pieces or shred.
3. Cut sausage into pieces.
4. Wrap in the tortilla.
5. Heat in microwave for 30-40 seconds.

~~Ronda

Peanut Butter Oatmeal

INGREDIENTS:
- One package of oatmeal, any flavor or plain
- Milk
- Peanut butter

DIRECTIONS:
1. Follow package directions to make oatmeal.
2. Half-way through cooking, add peanut butter and stir.
3. Add milk and eat!

"Getcha fiber and protein at once! Now that's smart eating"!

~~Lataurus

Snacks

To Changed Choices staff and volunteers: From my heart to yours because you give me hope. I look forward to knowing what you are able to do with these recipes.

~~Renée

The staff and volunteers at Changed Choices are my new family and friends. They believe in me when everyone else has given up on me. They are all angels that God has sent to help us find our way and to remind us often that we are loved, we are not alone, we are going to make it through this.

~~Chanteil

Cream Cheese Balls

INGREDIENTS:
- 1 package cookies – Oreo
- 1 jar cream cheese
- 3 Tbsp. Creamer

DIRECTIONS:
1. Separate cookies, putting the filling into a bowl.
2. Crumble the cookies and divide into two piles.
3. Add same amount of cream cheese as there is the cookie filling in your bowl.
4. Add 3 Tbsp. creamer and mix until smooth.
5. Add one pile of crumbled cookies and mix.
6. Roll into balls. They should be firm enough but if not, add more cookies.
7. Drop balls into the second pile of cookie crumbles and roll to coat with cookie crumbles. Give them another palm roll and place on cookie sheet.
8. Refrigerate for at least 6 hours.

Note: To change the flavor of your filling, you can add one single-use packet of Kool-Aid to the cream cheese.

Enjoy!

~~LaChelle

Peanut Butter Balls

Makes 10-12 balls

INGREDIENTS:

- ½ jar peanut butter
- ½ cup crushed peanuts
- ¾ cup crushed pretzels and/or vanilla cookies
- 1 Hershey bar

DIRECTIONS:

1. Put peanut butter into bowl.
2. Add crushed pretzels and/or vanilla cookies.
3. Form into balls.
4. Roll balls in crushed nuts until completely coated.
5. Melt Hershey bar in microwave and drizzle over the balls.

~~Ronda

Deep Fried Pickles

INGREDIENTS:

- 2 packages ranch dressing
- Bag of potato chips
- Pickles
- Microwave safe plate

DIRECTIONS:

- Crush the potato chips.
- Slice the pickles.
- Dip pickle slices into ranch dressing and coat well.
- Roll the pickles in the potato chip crumbs.
- Place on microwave safe plate.
- Microwave for 2 minutes or until crispy.

~~Lisa

Popcorn Balls

Makes 8-10 balls

INGREDIENTS:

- 1 bag microwave popcorn
- 1 bag caramels
- 1 pack mayo

DIRECTIONS:

1. Microwave popcorn for 2 minutes.
2. Pour into medium trash bag.
3. Put caramels in a bowl or cup, add mayo, and microwave until melted.
4. Pour on top of popcorn in bag, and shake.
5. Roll into balls.

~~Ronda

Salsa

Serves 2-4 people

INGREDIENTS:
- 2 Pasta sauce packets
- 2 Apples, red
- 1 ½ pickle
- 1 chili noodle seasoning, or 2 packs for extra spicy

DIRECTIONS:
1. Mix chili powder and pasta sauce in a bowl.
2. Let sit for one day.
3. Dice the apple and put it into the pasta sauce.
4. Dice the pickle and add to the sauce.
5. Let sit for a day.
6. Check to see if it is too spicy. If you want it less spicy, add pickle juice.

Note: Very good with Cool Ranch Doritos

~~Corina

Sausage Snack

INGREDIENTS:

- 1 Summer Sausage
- 1 Block of any cheese
- 1 pickle
- Crackers (optional)

INSTRUCTIONS:

1. Slice each item.
2. Stack items, starting with the sausage, then cheese, then pickle.
3. If desired, you may stack these on a cracker!

~~Dravia

Taffy

INGREDIENTS:

- 1 cup coffee creamer (unflavored is best)
- 1 to 2 packets of any flavor drink mix

DIRECTIONS:

1. Mix the two ingredients together well.
2. Add about 2 to 3 teaspoons of very hot water. Mix until smooth.
3. Set aside. Consistency should be that of taffy – firm and tacky.

~~Deb

The staff and volunteers are the pillar of our happiness. The kindness that they bestow can only be measured by our smiles. There is no amount of money that can be paid to measure their worth.

~~Apryl

Main Dishes

By sharing our food recipes with staff and volunteers, we are giving back some of the joy that you have given us. We are giving you that gift of sharing ourselves as you have given it to us.

~~Ronda

I dedicate this to Changed Choices staff and volunteers because they are helping me change my life.

~~Teresa

Changed **Choices**

Building new lives beyond prison walls

Bang Bang Delight

INGREDIENTS:

- 1 package macaroni and cheese
- ½ bag of Four Cheese Idaho mashed potatoes
- Hamburger Steak
- Shredded or squeeze cheese

DIRECTIONS:

1. Mix the macaroni and cheese together, and then add the potatoes and hamburger steak.
2. Top with cheese.
3. Warm in microwave.

Unlimited calories! If you're on a diet, please do not try this at home ☺

~~Lataurus

Chili Cheese Chicken

INGREDIENTS:

- 8 pieces of fried chicken (from the canteen)
- I can of chili – with or without beans
- Cheese sauce (squeeze cheese)
- Shredded cheese

DIRECTIONS:

1. Remove chicken meat from the bone.
2. Save chicken skins on the side, breaking up into small pieces of skin.
3. Put chicken into a microwave safe bowl.
4. Add chili and cheese sauce – mix ingredients.
5. Smooth out the top.
6. Sprinkle shredded cheese on top.
7. Sprinkle chicken skin pieces over that.
8. Microwave for about 3 minutes until chicken skin is crunchy.

~~LaChelle

Mac-n-Cheese (with a twist)

INGREDIENTS:
- I pack pasta shells
- Squeeze cheese
- Ranch dressing
- Ramen noodles seasoning pack
- Optional – pepperoni, sausage, mayo

DIRECTIONS:
1. Boil water in microwave.
2. Add shells and cook until al dente.
3. Put cheese in another bowl, the more the better.
4. Add small amount of hot water and stir until smooth.
5. Add packet of ranch dressing and stir.
6. Add packet of seasoning from Ramen noodles to cheese sauce, and stir.
7. Add cheese sauce to pasta shells.

Optional – If meat is desired, add pepperoni or sausage.

Note – If cheese sauce is dry, add mayo. Cheese sauce should be consistent, but not runny.

~~Noria

Potato Roll Casserole

INGREDIENTS:
- 1 bag chips – any kind
- Block cheese
- Pepperoni roll

DIRECTIONS:
1. Crush chips well.
2. Add a little water to make a paste of the chips - not too dry or too wet.
3. Spread out to make a tortilla-like base.
4. Cut up block cheese and pepperoni into small pieces.
5. Spread cheese and pepperoni over the "paste" of chips.
6. Carefully roll the "paste" with the ingredients inside.
7. Microwave until crisp – check every minute to determine when it is crisp.
8. Cut it into slices and enjoy.

NOTE:
- Adding egg is optional; use the dried eggs according to directions.
- Squeeze cheese can be substituted for cut up block cheese.

~~Dravia

Prison Casserole

INGREDIENTS:

- Rice
- Beans
- Noodles
- Cheese
- Potato chips
- Summer Sausage
- Ramen
- Anything else you choose to include!

DIRECTIONS:

1. Mix everything together in a microwave-safe bowl.
2. Cover with squeeze cheese.
3. Microwave until warmed through.

~~Amanda

Thank you for your love, your encouragement, your wisdom and your friendship. Thank you, most of all, for joining me on my journey as I strengthen my friendship with JESUS CHRIST.

--*April*

Changed **Choices**
Building new lives beyond prison walls

Hispanic Cuisine

All staff and volunteers mean so much to me! The letters and the time you invest mean everything! The quotes, magazine clips etc. that you send are such an encouragement. Thank you!

~ ~ Corina

You don't know me but you reach out to me and are supportive of me. I am grateful for you.

~ ~ Kisameia

Easy Nachos

INGREDIENTS:

- Chili in a bag
- Squeeze cheese
- Ground beef
- Pickles
- Nacho chips
- Seasoning packs

DIRECTIONS:

- Arrange nachos along the bottom of a plate.
- Heat chili in a bowl for two minutes.
- Heat the ground beef in a separate bowl for 2 minutes.
- Mix seasoning in while heating each meat.
- Cut the pickle into small slices and set aside.
- Once the chili is hot, drain the grease and pour over the nachos.
- Sprinkle the ground beef over the chili.
- Cut a small slit in the corner of the squeeze cheese and drizzle on top of your creation!
- Sprinkle the pickles over the top for color and extra flavor.

Voila!

~~Apryl

Enchiladas

Serves: 1-4 people

INGREDIENTS:
- shredded pork, beef, or chicken (from box or canteen)
- 1 pasta sauce
- 2 squeeze cheese
- 1 package tortilla wraps
- 2 block cheese – provolone, cheddar, or mozzarella
- seasoning from a package of noodles
- salt and pepper

DIRECTIONS:
1. Put shredded meat in bowl with salt and pepper and small amount of seasoning from noodles.
2. In separate bowl put pasta sauce, one squeeze cheese, salt & pepper, and a tablespoon of water.
3. Stir until smooth and soupy, without lumps.
4. Place meat in the middle of the tortilla wrap on a plate.
5. Pour most of the soupy sauce on top of the meat and wrap like a burrito.
6. Grate the block cheese and pour most of it over the enchilada.
7. Add the remaining sauce and squeeze cheese on top ~ zig-zagging for decorative appearance.
8. Top with the remaining block cheese.
9. Microwave for 5 minutes.

Enjoy!

Note: If you are cooking for 4 people, use a puzzle 'box' and put trash bags to cover the top of the box and eat your enchiladas.

~~Corina

Nachos à la Renée

INGREDIENTS:

- 1 bag of chips – Doritos or Tostitos
- ½ pickle
- ½ package meat of your choice (beef, turkey, or sausage)
- Salsa
- Rice and beans or chili
- 1 pack of Ramen noodles
- Squeeze cheese

DIRECTIONS:

1. Cook Ramen noodles, following directions on pack.
2. Cook rice & beans or chili, following the directions on the pack.
3. Cut pickle into small slices.
4. Mix the noodles and rice & beans or chili together. If desired, add meat to the mixture.
5. Lay out the chips and place the noodles with rice & beans or chili over the top.
6. Add meat of choice, squeeze cheese, salsa, and pickle.

~~Renée

Nachos à la Teresa

INGREDIENTS:

- Doritos
- 1 package Ramen noodles – any flavor
- Can of chili with beans
- Squeeze cheese
- Summer sausage
- Pickle

INSTRUCTIONS:

1. Put noodles in a bowl. 'Cook' the noodles by adding hot water and allow them to swell.
2. Add seasoning packet.
3. Heat the chili with beans in microwave, then pour over the noodles.
4. Chop the summer sausage and add to the noodle and chili mixture.
5. Spread the Doritos on a plate and cover with the mixture.
6. Dice the pickle, sprinkling the pieces over the mixture.
7. Squeeze the cheese over the top.

~~Teresa

Quesadillas

Makes 1-4 servings

INGREDIENTS
- 1 pack tortilla wraps
- Block cheese (approximately 2 blocks per person)
- Meat (optional)

DIRECTIONS:
1. Cut block cheese in julienne cut.
2. Put cheese on one side of tortilla wrap.
3. Add your meat of preference.
4. Fold tortilla to cover cheese and meat.
5. Microwave for 2 ½ minutes.

Enjoy!

~~Corina

Taco Bowl

INGREDIENTS:
- I pack of wraps
- 2 squeeze cheese
- 2 ranch dressing
- I block cheese, any kind, shredded
- I bag Doritos or Fritos
- I pack ground beef or taco filling
- Optional ~ One pack rice or noodles

DIRECTIONS:
1. Put each wrap in small bowl and microwave until hard and bowl-shaped.
2. Put layer of Fritos or Doritos on bottom.
3. Build layers out of ground beef, cheese, and rice or noodles.
4. Top with Doritos or Fritos, shredded block cheese and ranch dressing.

~~Ronda

Tacos

INGREDIENTS:

- 1 Pack shredded beef or pork
- 1 Pack flour tortilla wraps
- 2 Packs squeeze cheese
- 2 Packs ranch dressing
- 2 Cups salsa
- 1 Pickle, diced
- 1 Bag refried beans and rice

Also needed: 4 paper plates

DIRECTIONS

1. Poke holes into tortillas with a fork or spork for ventilation
2. Fold 2 paper plates in half.
3. Place one wrap on top of one plate, placing a second paper plate of top of wrap, folding wrap over it and sealing.
4. Microwave for 1 minute and 15 seconds, or until wrap is crisp. Set aside and repeat with the other 4 wraps.
5. Place squeeze cheese in hot water to warm.
6. In separate bowls add water to refried beans and rice as directed on packages.
7. Put shredded beef in bowl and heat in microwave.
8. Assemble tacos into the crisp wrap: Refried beans and rice, shredded beef or chicken, cheese, pickle, and salsa. Top with ranch dressing.

~~Deb

Tamale à la Corina

INGREDIENTS:

- Bag of chips, Doritos or Fritos
- 1 Package shredded pork or beef.
- 1 Squeeze cheese
- Salt and pepper, or Ramen noodle seasoning for the meat

DIRECTIONS:

1. Crush the chips.
2. Mix in 1 cup of hot water, or more, until consistency is like dough.
3. Cut paper trash bag to 5x10 or 8x10.
4. Place dough on paper and flatten.
5. Add seasoned shredded meat, then the squeeze cheese to the middle of the dough.
6. Fold the sides in first, and then the ends, to create a burrito-shape.
7. Put in microwave for 2 minutes.

Enjoy!

~~Corina

Tamale à la Renée

INGREDIENTS:

- 4 small bags Fritos or Doritos
- 2 small bags pork rinds
- 1 hot sausage
- 1 cup of salsa
- 1 bag of precooked beans
- 4 packs of squeeze cheese
- 4 packs of chili seasoning (from Ramen noodles)
- 1 hot pickle, diced

Also Needed: 1 empty cookie tray from duplex cookies

DIRECTIONS:

1. Crush bags of Fritos or Doritos.
2. Mix 2 packs chili seasoning in one cup hot water.
3. Mix the seasoned water with the chips to make the masa (dough). Set aside.
4. Crush bags of pork rinds.
5. Mix sausage, pork rinds, and salsa together.
6. Cook beans in hot water.
7. Mix all cheese with the diced pickle and add small amount of seasoning.
8. Fill sides and bottom of cookie tray with masa.
9. In the center of the masa spread some beans and the sausage mix. (You can add additional pickle to make hotter.)
10. Put another layer of masa over the top, making sure the meat and beans are fully covered by masa.
11. Flip the cookie tray over and cover the tamales with cheese sauce.

Enjoy it!

~~Renée

The ladies at Changed Choices are amazing women and deserve to be thanked for how they have reached out to follow the Changed Choices ladies with their prayers and encouragement. And for me, they walked me through my journey, helping me to stay strong and not letting me give up and helping me to stay focused on what I needed to do which is staying in the guidelines of trusting God.

~~Lisa

Italian Cuisine

Thank you for all the hard work and dedication you give to help us grow to be women of God. Also for the prayers, thoughtful words and work you provide for our benefit.

~~Shirley

Thank you to all the staff and volunteers from Changed Choices for the letters, prayers, cards, love and encouragement that I have received since I have been a part of the organization. The Christmas gifts also meant so very much!

~~JoAnn

Building new lives beyond prison walls

Calzone

INGREDIENTS:

- 2 tortilla wraps
- 1 bag chili with beans
- 4.4 oz. rice
- 1 bag taco filling
- ½ bag mashed potatoes
- 1 squeeze cheese – jalapeño or regular

DIRECTIONS:

1. Microwave tortilla wraps 10 seconds to soften.
2. Fill wraps with chili with beans, rice, taco filling, and mashed potatoes.
3. Top with cheese and microwave to melt.

Unlimited calories!

~~Lataurus

Calzone Triple Decker

INGREDIENTS:

- 1 pack tortilla wraps
- Pepperoni
- Squeeze cheese
- 1 pasta sauce
- 1 block mozzarella cheese, cut julienne style
- 1 sausage

DIRECTIONS:

1. With tortilla laid flat on the surface, spread pasta sauce and squeeze cheese, to taste.
2. On one side of tortilla place pepperoni and block cheese julienne strips.
3. Place another tortilla on top, and repeat step 1.
4. On opposite side of tortilla place pepperoni or sausage.
5. Repeat step 1 again.
6. Repeat step 4, then fold in half.
7. Put in microwave for 2 ½ to 3 minutes. If you want it crunchy, place in popcorn bag.

Enjoy!

~~Corina

Cold Pasta

INGREDIENTS:

- Noodles – any kind
- Ranch dressing
- Duke's mayo
- Olives or pickles, according to preference
- Vegetable flakes
- 2 of any meats (tuna, sausage, pepperoni)
- Block cheese

DIRECTIONS:

1. Cook noodles and allow them to cool completely.
2. Rinse noodles completely with cold water and let them sit in cold water.
3. Cut up the meat, block cheese, and pickles and/or olives.
4. Drain the noodles. Mix the ranch dressing and the mayo into the noodles, making them creamy.
5. Mix the meat, olive or pickles, and vegetable flakes into the noodles.
6. Add salt and pepper to taste.

This is #2 of my favorite prison recipes...

~~Bianca

Lasagna

INGREDIENTS:

- 1 pack wraps
- 2 squeeze cheese, cheddar
- 1 block cheese, any kind
- 1 pasta sauce
- 1 package noodles
- 1 pack ground beef or lasagna meat
- 1 pack mayo

DIRECTIONS:

1. Grease bottom of large bowl with mayo.
2. Cut tortilla wraps in triangles to layer easily in bowl.
3. Cook noodles and drain.
4. Shred block cheese.
5. Add small amount of hot water to squeeze cheese to make cheese sauce.
6. Mix pasta sauce in ground beef or with lasagna mixture.
7. Layer in bowl, alternating noodles, wraps, meat mixture, and cheeses.
8. Cook in microwave until thoroughly heated – about 4 or 5 minutes.
9. Optional ~ top with ranch.

~~Ronda

Lasagna with Sausage

INGREDIENTS:

- 1 pack of six 8-inch flour tortillas
- 8 ounces ground beef, season and brown
- 1 pack sliced pepperoni
- One 5-ounce summer sausage, diced
- 1 block cheddar cheese, grated
- 1 block Pepper Jack or Mozzarella cheese, grated
- 2 packs squeeze cream cheese (or 4 oz.)
- 2 packs squeeze cheddar cheese or 4-ounce cup cheddar cheese
- 3 packs pasta sauce or 18-ounce jar pizza or spaghetti sauce

Also need: 1-quart plastic microwave-safe bowl

DIRECTIONS:

1. Cut each tortilla into 4 triangles.
2. Put the 4 triangle tortillas on bottom of bowl. Will overlap slightly.
3. Cover tortillas with layer of pasta sauce, and then cover with layer of ground beef.
4. Squeeze one pack of cream cheese (or 2 ounces) on top of beef.
5. Put 4 triangles of tortillas on top.
6. Cover with layer of pasta sauce.
7. Put layer of diced sausage on top of sauce.
8. Cover with layer of squeeze or cup cheese.
9. Put 4 tortilla triangles on top.
10. Cover with layer of pasta sauce
11. Place layer of sliced pepperoni on top of sauce.
12. Cover with both kinds of grated cheese.
13. Repeat steps 2-12.
14. Heat in microwave for 5-6 minutes.
15. Let stand a few minutes.
16. Cut and serve.
17. Optional ~ Top with ranch.

~~Amy

Pasta Salad

INGREDIENTS

- Pasta shells
- 1 Pickle
- 1 Summer sausage
- 1 block cheese, any type
- Ranch dressing
- Pepperoni, sliced

DIRECTIONS

1. Cook the pasta according to package instructions and drain.
2. Chop the pickle, summer sausage, cheese, and pepperoni.
3. Mix all ingredients and add ranch dressing to your desired consistency.

Note: The pasta salad is good cold and will keep for several days refrigerated.

~~Dravia

Pizza

INGREDIENTS:

- Package of 6 flour tortillas
- 2 packages of mayo
- 1 package of sliced pepperoni
- 2 packs of pasta or pizza sauce
- One 5-ounce summer sausage, sliced
- 2 blocks of any kind cheese, shredded with forks
- 3 tablespoons cup cheese or 1 package
- 1 pack of green or black olives, sliced

DIRECTIONS:

- Mix the 3 tablespoons of cup cheese with the pasta sauce and set aside.
- Put mayo on a tortilla, rubbing another tortilla on it.
- Poke holes in the tortilla with a fork.
- Cook in the microwave for 1 to 1 ½ minutes. As it cools it will become hard. Repeat with the other tortillas.
- Cover with the pasta sauce and cup cheese mixture.
- Place a layer of sliced pepperoni on each tortilla.
- Place diced sausage on a paper towel and cook in microwave.
- Place layer of sausage on top of pepperoni.
- Cover with a combination of grated cheeses.
- Cover with sliced olives.
- Cook each pizza individually in microwave for 30 – 45 seconds.
- Optional: Put ranch over top before eating.

Eat and enjoy!

~~Amy

Spaghetti

INGREDIENTS:

- Package of Ramen noodles – any flavor
- Pasta sauce
- Summer sausage
- Squeeze cheese
- Pepperoni

INSTRUCTIONS:

1. Cook Ramen noodles, then add seasoning packet.
2. Add pasta sauce to noodles.
3. Chop summer sausage and add it to the noodles.
4. Put into a bowl and top with pepperoni.
5. Squeeze the cheese over the top!

~~Teresa

Oriental Cuisine

With appreciation we dedicate this wonderful cookbook that has been created by valued, beautiful and talented women in Changed Choices to you, the staff and volunteers. You mean so much to us for giving the dedication and strength through your love and prayers. God has a wonderful plan for each and every one of us and this is just one of the many.

~~Stephanie

I appreciate all the staff and volunteers who send letters, Bible Studies, prayers and for your concern for me. These recipes are just a taste of what we have here! Hopefully someday soon, I will be out and will be able to be a volunteer. Volunteers keep this organization alive!

~~Bianca

Changed **Choices**
Building new lives beyond prison walls

Fried Rice

- 1 bag dried eggs
- 1 bag of rice
- 1 summer sausage
- 2 packs mayo (or grease from sausage if preferred)
- 1 seasoning pack from Ramen noodles, any flavor

DIRECTIONS:
1. Pour rice in large bowl.
2. Coat rice with mayo, and then sprinkle the seasoning over the top.
3. Chop summer sausage into small pieces and heat in microwave.
4. Pour grease over rice, if not using mayo.
5. Heat rice in microwave in 20-second intervals, for around two minutes or until toasty. Stir to keep from burning. Let cool.
6. Add hot water to eggs, set aside until fluffy.
7. Add water to just cover the rice, cook approximately 3 minutes. Let sit until tender.
8. Add meat, then eggs and toss together.
9. Heat for additional 1 to 2 minutes.
10. Serve it as is, or put it into a wrap.
11. Option: Add honey mustard sauce.

Enjoy! ☺

~~Deb

Fried Rice à la Bianca

INGREDIENTS
- White rice
- Seasoning, beef flavor
- Cola
- Meat, any kind (sausage, pepperoni, chicken)
- Grated Block cheese
- Ranch or Duke's mayo
- Vegetable flakes

DIRECTIONS
1. Add rice to bowl with seasoning, ranch (1 pack), and mayo (2 packs).
2. Microwave rice mixture for 60 seconds.
3. Remove bowl and stir rice. Microwave for another 30 to 40 seconds, continuing until rice is brown.
4. Allow the bowl to cool for 1 minute, and then add cola to the bowl until the rice is covered.
5. Add the block cheese, chopped meat, and vegetable flakes.
6. Microwave for 5 to 6 minutes.
7. Optional: Put ranch dressing or squeeze cheese over top.

~~*Bianca*

Fried Teriyaki Rice

INGREDIENTS:

- I 20-ounce Pepsi
- I heaping tablespoon instant coffee (Columbian)
- I 8-ounce bag of long-grain rice
- I 5-ounce summer sausage, diced
- I pack Ramen noodle seasoning, any flavor
- 2 tablespoons mayo

Also needed: Quart-sized microwave sized bowl

DIRECTIONS:

- Place rice, seasoning, mayo, and diced sausage, in bowl. DO NOT add water.
- Stir together, then heat in microwave for 45 seconds.
  - Remove, stir, and heat an additional 45 seconds.
  - Remove, stir, and heat another 45 seconds.
  - Remove, stir, and heat for 30 seconds.
- Add tablespoon of coffee.
- Add Pepsi until it covers the rice.
- Cook in microwave for 6 minutes.
- Let stand for 5 minutes and serve.

~~Amy

Thai Noodle Chips

INGREDIENTS

- 1 bag of Thai Palace rice noodles
- Mayo

DIRECTIONS

1. Place noodles in microwave-safe bowl. Add mayo and stir until noodles are coated.
2. Put noodles in microwave for approximately 1 minute.
3. Take them out and stir in the noodle seasoning packet completely.
4. Put back into the microwave, stirring every 30 seconds. The noodles should be crisp, but not burn.
5. Remove noodles and cool.

~~Dravia

Seafood

When I think about the staff at Changed Choices, Hebrews 13:3 comes to mind. It says "Continue to remember those in prison as if you were together with them in prison". The staff at Changed Choices is truly amazing and God sent. Thank You!

~~Kamie

I would like to dedicate this book to the awesome staff at Changed Choices. You all take time out of a busy schedule to pray for us and our families. You show us in so many ways that not only are we loved but we are not alone. Thank you with love.

~~LaChelle

Fish Patties

INGREDIENTS:

- 1 package of fish – use salmon, tuna, or mackerel
- 6 Packs of mayo
- 2 small bags of The Whole Shabang chips
- 1 seasoning packet from Ramen noodles – any flavor

INSTRUCTIONS:

1. Drain fish.
2. Blend fish with 3 or 4 packs of mayo.
3. Crush 1 bag of chips and mix in with fish.
4. Mold the mixture into patties.
5. Blend remaining mayo with second bag of chips.
6. Coat the patties with the mayo/chips mixture.
7. Place patties on the lid of the microwave-safe bowl and microwave for two minutes until crispy.
8. Cool on paper towels.

Enjoy!

~~Dawn

Salmon Patties

INGRÉDIENTS:

- 2 packs of salmon (tuna or mackerel may be used)
- A couple packs of crackers or a handful of potato chips
- 2 packs of mayo, or 1 pack of ranch

DIRECTIONS

1. Mix fish in a bowl with crushed crackers or chips, and mayo or ranch.
2. Shape into patties.
3. Microwave on each side until crisp and firm.

~~Ronda

Tuna and Sausage with Noodles

INGREDIENTS:

- 1 package Ramen noodles – any flavor
- ½ of a 1-ounce bag instant rice
- 1 can tuna
- 1 kielbasa sausage – chopped small
- Shredded cheese
- Seasoning salt

FOR CHEESE SAUCE

- 2 teaspoons mustard
- 1 ½ tablespoon mayo
- Squeeze cheese

INSTRUCTIONS:

1. In a microwave-safe bowl, layer noodles (without noodle seasoning), tuna, rice, sausage, shredded cheese, and seasoning salt.
2. Repeat until all ingredients are used.
3. Add water just until layers are covered.
4. Microwave for 5 to 7 minutes.
5. In the meantime, make cheese sauce by combining mustard, mayo, noodle seasoning, and squeeze cheese until creamy.
6. Cool noodle bowl for 15 minutes, and then pour cheese sauce over the top.

~~Veronica

Tuna Casserole

INGREDIENTS:

- 1 package Ramen noodles – any flavor
- 1 package tuna, drained
- 5 mayo packets
- 1 small block of cheddar cheese, grated or chopped into small chunks

INSTRUCTIONS:

- Make the noodles according to instructions.
- Mix in the mayo packets and tuna.
- Mix in your cheese, leaving a nice layer for the top.
- Microwave until cheese is melted on top.

ENJOY!

Note: You can add cooked vegetables of any kind to give this dish some pizazz!

~~Dravia

Tuna Pasta

INGREDIENTS:

- 1 package tuna
- 1 bag pasta shells, cooked as directed
- 1 pickle
- 1 block mozzarella cheese
- 6 packages mayo
- 1 package ranch
- Tortillas or club crackers

DIRECTIONS:

1. Cut mozzarella into small chunks.
2. Mix the first 6 ingredients together in a microwave-safe bowl.
3. Heat until warmed through.
4. Eat with tortillas or crackers.

~~Latasha

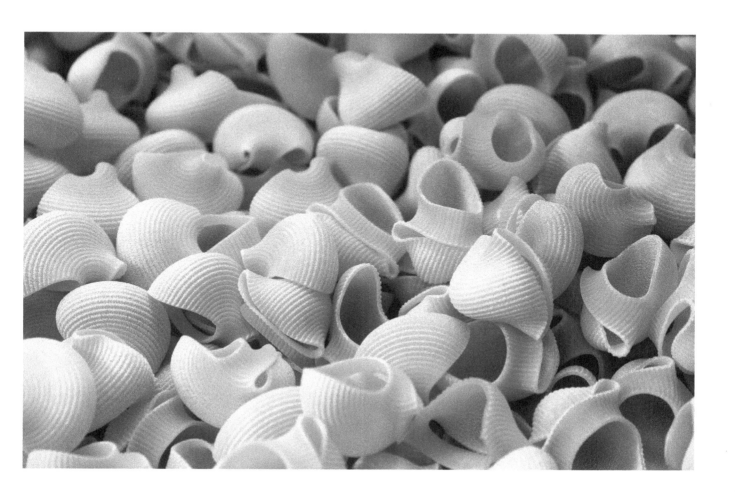

These recipes are a small way to thank you for everything that you do for us.

~ ~*Dawn*

Desserts

The staff and volunteers mean so much. To hear that the ladies are praying for us, sending us Bible verses etc. makes you feel good all over! It lifts me up! We want to share a little of our lives here with all of you out there!

~~Amanda

Nothing beats a good meal to sanctify and nourish our bodies because its warm, comforting, it fulfills and sustains, much like the love we receive from each member of the Changed Choices team, staff and volunteers alike. This collaboration is dedicated to you and at such times of separation, what a fabulous way to enjoy a meal together. Recipes are cherished, passed down and hold much meaning to those whose lineage it comes from. So from our table to yours, may your plates always be full and your souls never empty.

~~Alisha

Changed Choices
Building new lives beyond prison walls

Cake

INGREDIENTS:

- 1 large pack cookies or 4 small packs, any variety (you may add cake or cookies from dining room)
- 2 packs mayo
- 1-2 packs cream cheese
- 1 pack peanut butter
- 2 packs hot chocolate
- Optional ~ candy bars, caramels, peppermint bark

DIRECTIONS:

1. Separate cookies, saving cream in a separate bowl. This will be used for the icing.
2. Crush cookies as finely as possible.
3. Add any leftover cake or cookies after crushing.
4. Put ½ to 1 cream cheese and 1 pack mayo into mixture.
5. Add hot water until able to stir.
6. Grease a separate bowl with mayo and pour mixture into it.
7. Microwave 4 or 5 minutes, until sides pull away from bowl.
8. Invert onto lid or piece of cardboard.

ICING THE CAKE:

1. Take cream from cookies, remaining cream cheese, peanut butter, hot chocolate, melted Hershey bar, if available, and put into bowl. Heat in microwave, stirring, until creamy.
2. Optional ~ Add candy bars, peppermint bark, etc. Drizzle with melted caramel.
3. Optional ~ Make a 2-layer cake by using a piece of dental floss to cut cake when cooled. Put icing in the middle.

~~Ronda

Ice Cream Cone

INGREDIENTS:

- 1 pint ice cream, any flavor
- 2 flour tortillas
- 2 small packs sugar (optional)
- 1 chocolate candy bar
- 1 cup of crushed cookies
- 4 pieces of paper
- 4 small pieces of tape

DIRECTIONS:

1. Using a spork, poke holes in each flour tortilla (This ventilates the tortilla so that it does not bubble up).
2. Lightly wet tortilla with water.
3. Roll each sheet of paper into a cone shape.
4. Place one tortilla over the paper cone, shaping it.
5. Place second cone on top of the tortilla.
6. Repeat steps 4 and 5 to make second cone.
7. Microwave in an upright position for 1 minute and 15 seconds to make crispy.
   Note: You may need to make something to hold the cone upright before microwaving
8. While the cones cool, crush the cookies.
9. Break a small piece of chocolate and place at the bottom of the cone to make a delicious 'plug'.
10. Microwave the rest of the candy bar in the microwave at 7-second intervals, stirring so it does not burn.
11. Using a spork, paint the inside of each cone with chocolate. Set aside to cool.
12. Layer ice cream, then the crushed cookies, inside each cone, ending with crushed cookies

Enjoy your ice cream cone quickly ~ because it will melt!

~~Deb

Lava Cake

INGREDIENTS
- 2 puddings
- 5 Oreo cookies
- Creamer, French vanilla or regular
- Small amount of mayo

Also Needed: Small bowl with lid

DIRECTIONS:
1. Separate the Oreo cookies and save filling for icing.
2. Crush the cookies to a fine consistency and put into a bowl.
3. Put the icing in a separate bowl.
4. Mix the pudding with the Oreos until it is a paste.
5. Use a spoon to pack the paste tightly inside the bowl.
6. Mix the icing with a drop of mayo, a sprinkle of creamer, and most of the pudding.
7. Spread pudding mixture over the packed cookie paste.
8. Put the lid on the bowl and place it in boiling water for 10 minutes.
9. Let cool for 10 minutes and enjoy!

~~Candice

Quick Microwave Cookies

INGREDIENTS:
- Oatmeal
- Hot Chocolate
- Peanut Butter
- ½ bag plain M&M's, optional

Also Needed: Plastic bags and Plates

DIRECTIONS:
1. Mix 4 packs of plain oatmeal and 1 ½ tablespoons of peanut butter into a bowl with just enough warm water to make a thick mixture.
2. Add one package of hot chocolate.
3. Roll mixture into a ball, and then flatten it onto the plastic bag.
4. Separate into 6 or 8 cookies.
5. Add M&M's, if desired.
6. Put only two cookies at a time on the plate and put into microwave for 1 ½ minutes.

Enjoy!

~~Apryl

State Cake

INGREDIENTS:

- 1 large package of cookies with cream filling – any flavor
- 2 honey buns, preferably glazed
- 1 package of cream cheese
- ¼ cup creamer – either liquid or powder
- 3 packets of Duke's mayo

INSTRUCTIONS:

1. Separate the cookies, scraping off the cream center into a bowl.
2. Crush the cookies into a powdery mixture.
3. Mix the cream cheese, the creamer, and the cookie cream together.
4. Add milk or water as needed, to get an icing consistency.
5. Split the crushed cookie powder in half.
6. Add milk or water to one half, mixing well until it is moistened; then mix in 3 packets of mayo.
7. Using a microwave-safe bowl put this mixture in the bottom of the bowl.
8. Flatten a honey bun and use it as the next layer.
9. Cover with some of the icing mix and a layer of crumbles.
10. Top with the second honey bun, flattened.
11. Cover with the remaining icing, and then sprinkle with the remaining crumbs.
12. Microwave for two minutes, cool, and EAT!

~~Dawn

Tiramisu

INGREDIENTS:

- 1 pack Oreo or Double-Stuff Oreo cookies
- 3 tablespoons instant coffee, Columbian
- 3 bags square caramels
- 4 packs squeeze cream cheese
- 1 tablespoon mayo
- A few shakes of powdered creamer

Also needed: Quart-sized microwave safe bowl

DIRECTIONS:

1. Mix coffee with water until it dissolves.
2. Place caramels and mayo in a bowl with a couple spoons full of water and cook in microwave until melted. Stir frequently so it does not burn.
3. Once melted, put the cream cheese in the caramel mixture with a few shakes of creamer (for thickness). Blend thoroughly.
4. Dip each cookie in the coffee mixture, and then place a layer on the bottom of the bowl until covered.
5. Spoon cream cheese mixture over the layer of cookies until covered.
6. Place another layer of coffee-soaked cookies on top of cream cheese mixture.
7. Place another layer of cream cheese mixture on top of the cookies.
8. Repeat layering, finishing off with the cream cheese mixture.
9. Cover the bowl and let sit for several hours.

Eat and enjoy!

~~Amy

Afterword

The CARE I Women are a part of Changed Choices, an organization located in Charlotte NC. They are an incredible group of women who have experienced challenges but are determined to make the changes needed and to work for the life that God has for them. The CARE (**C**omprehensive **A**pproach to **R**e-**E**ntry) Program has two parts: CARE I made up of women who are incarcerated and CARE II consisting of women who have transitioned out of prison. Changed Choices holistically and comprehensively serves women throughout incarceration and re-entry, providing many services for their clients as they fulfill the mission of the organization, which reads:

"As followers of Christ, we empower currently and recently incarcerated women to achieve lasting, positive change through programming and personalized mental, emotional, physical and spiritual support."

The success of the women involved is due to their hard work and the character qualities they develop. Encouraging them along the way are seven dedicated staff members and about 250 volunteers who give tirelessly of their time to encourage the women through teaching a wide range of classes, facilitating Bible Studies, card writing, mentoring, being a pen pal, serving as members of the Board of Directors and endless ways behind the scenes. As a result, Changed Choices experiences a very low recidivism rate for their clients.

Although CARE I and II are the core programs of Changed Choices, the organization is very involved with the women at the local detention center. There, Changed Choices provides a mentoring program, teaches classes, (under contract), provides Bible Studies and has a strong professional counseling program that provides counseling to the residents.

The CARE II Program continues the work begun in CARE I with goal setting, case management and assisting the women in their new life. Re-entry support may include professional counseling, mentoring, physical provision, transportation assistance, affordable housing, and job search assistance, referrals to community partners and micro grants designed to propel clients toward living wage employment.

The relationships established are long lasting. The Changed Choices "family" develops ties that continue for years and include the families of the clients as well. Clients, client families, staff, volunteers, board members and faithful supporters are all a part of the Changed Choices family!

www.ChangedChoices.org
P.O. Box 34367
Charlotte, NC 28234

The staff and volunteers at Changed Choices mean a lot to me. They are a great support system and have constantly showed me that. They show much love through their cards and letters and it has been helpful to me many times. The staff and volunteers at Changed Choices are awesome.

~ ~ Rece

Changed **Choices**
Building new lives beyond prison walls

CPSIA information can be obtained
at www.ICGtesting.com
Printed in the USA
JSHW012010130521
14710JS00003B/43